The House of
the Seven Gables

NATHANIEL HAWTHORNE

Level 1

Retold by Michael Mendenhall
Series Editors: Andy Hopkins and Jocelyn Potter

Pearson Education Limited
Edinburgh Gate, Harlow,
Essex CM20 2JE, England
and Associated Companies throughout the world.

ISBN: 978-1-4058-4279-2

First published 1851
First published by Penguin Books 1981
This edition published 2008

5 7 9 10 8 6

Text copyright © Penguin Books 2000
This edition copyright © Pearson Education Ltd 2008
Illustrations copyright © Victor Ambrus 2000

Typeset by Graphicraft Ltd, Hong Kong
Set in 12/14pt Bembo
Printed in China
SWTC/05

Published by Pearson Education Ltd in association with
Penguin Books Ltd, both companies being subsidiaries of Pearson Plc

For a complete list of the titles available in the Penguin Readers series please write to your
local Pearson Longman office or to: Penguin Readers Marketing Department, Pearson
Education, Edinburgh Gate, Harlow, Essex CM20 2JE, England.

Introduction

"Oh, you didn't get my letter!" Phoebe said. "I want to visit you for a week or two."

"Let's talk about it," Hepzibah said. "This house is cold and dark. You're young. It's not the right place for you."

Hepzibah Pyncheon is an old woman, and she has money problems. She is opening a small store, and Phoebe, her young cousin, wants to work for her. One morning, Hepzibah's sick brother suddenly walks into the kitchen in the House of the Seven Gables. But where did he come from? Why was he away from home for thirty years? And why does Judge Pyncheon want to talk to him?

Nathaniel Hawthorne (1804–64) is a very famous American writer. He lived in New England with his two sisters and his mother. He was a good student, and later he had a good job in an office. But Hawthorne wanted to write stories about people in their new, young country. Americans were not British or European, but what were they? What were their problems? How did they think? What was in their hearts? What was right or wrong for them? Hawthorne thought about these questions.

Hawthorne finished four important books in the 1850s: *The Scarlet Letter*, *The House of the Seven Gables*, *The Blithedale Romance*, and *The Marble Faun*. In these books, he answers his difficult questions about people. He writes about good people and bad people, happy days and unhappy days. Many people read Hawthorne's books today because he teaches us about Americans at an important time in the story of the United States.

It was a dark old house.

Chapter 1   The Store

Miss Hepzibah Pyncheon lived in the House of the Seven Gables, on Pyncheon Street. It was a dark old house. There was a small room in the front gable and today, for the first time in many years, that room was a store again.

Hepzibah did not want to work in the store. It was very difficult for her. The people in the town did not like her. She was old, and her face was not beautiful. But she needed money. She needed food!

She went into the store and her first customer arrived. It was young Mr. Holgrave! He lived in one of the seven gables. He took pictures, usually of people's faces. Hepzibah started to cry.

"Ah, Mr. Holgrave, I cannot do this. I'm old, and only a woman. My father and mother and sister are dead. I want to go too."

"Oh, no!" the young man answered. "This is a good day for the Pyncheons. I can say that because we're friends."

Holgrave wanted some biscuits, but Hepzibah did not take any money from her only friend. Holgrave went away with his biscuits, and Hepzibah started to cry again.

"People here are cold," she thought. "They aren't going to buy from me."

Then the door opened again. It was only a little schoolboy. He asked for a biscuit from the window. Hepzibah did not take any money from her customer.

1

But then he came back and asked again for a biscuit! This time Hepzibah took his money. She needed it. But that morning Hepzibah did not make a lot of money.

In the afternoon, a man stopped in Pyncheon Street. He looked at the old house, and at the store window. He smiled at Hepzibah. It was her cousin, Judge Pyncheon!

Hepzibah did not love her cousin. He had a cold face, and she did not like his smile. She was afraid of him.

She went into a room at the back of the house and looked at an old picture of Colonel Pyncheon. He had the same cold face! Why did he build the House of the Seven Gables? He took the land for the house from Matthew Maule, the wizard. Then Maule cursed the Colonel and his family. The Colonel finished his house, but he was dead in his chair the same day! Was it the wizard's curse?

There was a customer in the store again. It was an old man with white hair. Mr. Venner did little jobs for people. He was slow, but he was smart about many things.

"You're working, Hepzibah! This is good," Mr. Venner said. "Smile for the customers. It's important!"

But she was an unhappy person, in an unhappy house.

Then Mr. Venner asked her, "When is he coming home?"

"*Who* is coming home?" Hepzibah said, with a white face.

"Ah, you don't want to talk about it. Then, goodbye."

That afternoon Hepzibah had many customers, but she did not make a lot of money. The schoolboy came again and asked for biscuits.

"Take them," she said. Then she closed the store.

Why did he build the House of the Seven Gables?

At the same time, a bus stopped on Pyncheon Street. A young girl said goodbye to the driver and went to the front door of the house. Hepzibah watched her.

"Who is it?" she thought. The girl was young and happy. She was at the door of the House of the Seven Gables, but she was not afraid.

Hepzibah opened the door. It was her little cousin Phoebe, from the country!

"Cousin Phoebe! Come in! What are you doing here?"

"Oh, you didn't get my letter!" Phoebe said. "I want to visit you for a week or two."

"Let's talk about it," Hepzibah said. "This house is cold and dark. You're young. It's not the right place for you."

"Cousin Hepzibah, maybe you're right. But I want to work and do things for you," Phoebe said.

"Yes, you're a good girl," Hepzibah answered. "I'm going to ask the man of the house about this."

"Who is that?" Phoebe asked.

"Did you never hear of Clifford Pyncheon?" Hepzibah asked. "He's my brother!"

"I know the name," Phoebe answered. "But he's dead!"

"Maybe he was," Hepzibah said. "But in this old house dead people can come back again!"

Chapter 2   Phoebe at Home

The morning light came into Phoebe's bedroom. She went to the window and looked down at the garden.

"Those white flowers are very beautiful," she thought. She went down to the garden, and she took some flowers back to her room. "Now this bedroom is mine," she thought.

She opened her door and started to go down again. Hepzibah called to her.

"Phoebe! Come into my room! Look at this."

Phoebe went in and Hepzibah opened her hand. Phoebe looked at a very small picture of a beautiful young man.

"He has a child's face!" Phoebe said.

The old woman started to cry.

"Don't cry, Cousin," Phoebe said. "Come, let's go to the kitchen."

In the kitchen, Hepzibah was quiet. Phoebe worked well.

"I can hear a customer in the store," Hepzibah said.

"Can I go, Cousin, please?" Phoebe asked.

"You, child!" Hepzibah said. "What can a country girl know about work in a store?"

But Hepzibah did not stop Phoebe. She watched her at work with a difficult customer. Phoebe finished and smiled.

"You can stay," Hepzibah said. "You're good in the house and good in the store, too!"

"Oh, thank you, Cousin Hepzibah!" Phoebe said.

Phoebe worked all day in the store. Customers came and went. Then they closed the store for the night.

Phoebe said, "Cousin, we need biscuits again, and people are asking for fruit. But look at our money!"

"You did well, Phoebe," Hepzibah said. "You're a good worker. The Pyncheons aren't good workers, because we have this house and land. But is it our land, or not?

5

"He has a child's face!" Phoebe said.

Colonel Pyncheon had the answer, but he's dead! Come with me, and you can see the Colonel's picture."

Phoebe went with her cousin. In the back room there was a picture of the Colonel, but she did not like his cold face.

Hepzibah talked about their family. One story was about beautiful Alice Pyncheon. Alice loved flowers, and people called the white flowers in the garden "Alice's Flowers." But Alice was sick, and in a short time she was dead. Was it the wizard's curse?

Then Hepzibah talked about Holgrave. "I like him," she said. "But sometimes I'm afraid of him."

"Afraid!" Phoebe said. "Then send him away."

"I can't," Hepzibah answered. "He's my only friend."

Phoebe wanted to go into the garden. She liked it because she was from the country. She looked at the beautiful flowers and trees.

"Who works in this garden?" Phoebe thought. "It isn't old Hepzibah," she said.

"It's me," a man behind her said.

Phoebe looked at the young man. "You?" Phoebe said.

"Yes. My name's Holgrave. I live in one of the seven gables, and I sometimes work in the garden. In my rooms in town I take pictures of people. I like taking pictures of their faces. Some faces are cold, but your face is a flower from this garden. Are you from the Pyncheon family?"

"My name is Phoebe Pyncheon," the girl said.

"What do you think of this picture?" Holgrave asked.

"I know that cold face," she answered.

repetition

Phoebe took a picture from his hand and looked at it. "I know that cold face," she answered. "It's Colonel Pyncheon in a new coat, and with no hat."

Holgrave smiled. "Look again," he said. "It's not Colonel Pyncheon. But you're going to meet this man one day."

"He has the same cold face," Phoebe said. "My cousin has a small picture of a beautiful young man. I like *his* face."

"Yes, Miss Hepzibah often talks about that picture," the young man said. "I want to see it, too. Did you see his unhappy eyes?"

"Unhappy?" Phoebe said. "He has the face of a child."

"Maybe," Holgrave said. "Maybe a bad child."

"How can you say that?" Phoebe said. "You don't know the picture!"

She started to go. "Wait!" Holgrave said. "There's a lot of work here, in the garden. Let's do it—you and I."

Phoebe worked with Holgrave. They stayed in the garden for a short time. Then it was dark.

"Good night, Miss Phoebe Pyncheon," Holgrave said. "One day, put a flower in your hair and come to my rooms in town. I want to take your picture."

Holgrave went into the house. Phoebe went in, too.

"Good night, Cousin," she said to Hepzibah.

"Good night, my child." Hepzibah kissed her.

"My cousin loves me very much," Phoebe thought. She went to bed, but that night she did not sleep well.

Chapter 3 Phoebe's Family

In the morning, Phoebe went down to the kitchen. Hepzibah smiled at her.

Phoebe started to make some coffee and hot food. She worked quickly, and in a short time it was on the table. There were flowers on the table, and three chairs.

"Why does she want three chairs?" Phoebe thought.

Then Hepzibah started to cry.

"Cousin, what's wrong?" Phoebe asked.

Hepzibah took her hand. "Oh, Phoebe, he's coming! Stand in front of the door. I'm old, but you're young and happy. Smile for him, Phoebe, smile. Sh–sh–sh! I can hear him. He's coming!"

There was a noise behind the door. Hepzibah opened it, and there was an old man with long hair. Phoebe looked at him. Was this the man in Hepzibah's picture? Was this the man with the face of a child?

"Clifford, this is our Cousin Phoebe," Hepzibah said slowly. "Little Phoebe Pyncheon—Arthur's only child, you know! She's visiting us from the country."

"Phoebe? Phoebe Pyncheon?" Clifford said. "I can't remember."

"Come, brother, sit in this chair," Hepzibah said. "Let's eat!"

Phoebe watched him. He moved very slowly and did not talk. But he liked his food! He smiled at Phoebe. "Yes," Phoebe thought. "It *is* the same man— Hepzibah's brother. But where did he come from?"

"Would you like some coffee?" Hepzibah asked him.

Clifford looked at Hepzibah's face. It was not beautiful.

Was this the man in Hepzibah's picture?

"Are you angry with me, Hepzibah?" he asked.

"Angry!" Hepzibah said. "Clifford, there's only love here. You're at home!"

Clifford smiled, but suddenly the light went from his eyes. Phoebe thought quickly.

"Cousin, here's a flower from your garden," she said.

"Ah, thank you!" Clifford said. "Ah, I remember this flower. Now I'm young again. But what's that noise?"

"Phoebe, please go and see our customer," Hepzibah said. "Clifford, we don't have much money. I opened a little store in the front gable. We need money for food."

"'We don't have much money,'" he said quietly, with a little smile. Then he closed his eyes and went to sleep.

Phoebe went into the store. It was the schoolboy again. This time he wanted one or two things for his mother. The boy went away with his bag. Then the door opened again. A fat man in an expensive black coat came in.

"This is an important man," Phoebe thought.

"Excuse me. I'm looking for Miss Hepzibah Pyncheon," he said. He smiled at Phoebe. "Do you work here?"

"Of course," Phoebe said. "But I'm Miss Hepzibah's cousin. I'm visiting her."

"Her cousin? And from the country? Are you Phoebe Pyncheon, the only child of my cousin Arthur? Do you know me, my child? I'm Judge Pyncheon, your cousin!"

He wanted to kiss Phoebe. He came near, but she moved back. "I don't want to kiss him," she thought. "But why?"

She looked up at his dark face. Suddenly she

"I don't want to kiss him," she thought.

remembered Holgrave's picture. This was the same man—the man with Colonel Pyncheon's face!

"What's wrong?" the Judge asked. "Are you afraid of me?"

"Oh, no, Cousin!" Phoebe answered. "But you want to talk to Cousin Hepzibah. I can get her for you."

"No, wait!" the Judge said. "What's wrong? Is there a visitor in this house? Are you afraid of him?"

"Oh, no!" Phoebe said. "There are no bad men in our house. There is only Cousin Hepzibah's brother. He isn't very well, but I'm not afraid of him."

"Not afraid?" the Judge said. "Then you don't know his story. He did a very bad thing. But we were friends. Is he here? I'm going to see."

"Wait, Cousin," Phoebe said. "Clifford's sleeping, I think. Let's ask Cousin Hepzibah first."

"No, no, Miss Phoebe!" the Judge said. He was angry. "I know the house well, and Hepzibah, and her brother Clifford. I want to talk to him—it's important. Remember, Phoebe, I'm at home here and you are the visitor. Ah! Here is Hepzibah!"

Hepzibah stopped at the door. She looked at the Judge. Her eyes were very small and cold.

"Hepzibah!" the Judge said, and smiled. "I'm very happy for you, and for us. Clifford is home! Can I see him now?"

"No," Hepzibah answered. "He cannot see visitors!"

"A visitor, Cousin? Do you call me a visitor? Please, come to my house in the country. Clifford can be happy there. Don't think about it—come!"

"Clifford has a home here!" Hepzibah said.

The Judge was angry. "Woman," he said, "why do you want to stay here? Do you have money? No! But why am I talking to you? You're only a woman! I want to see Clifford. Now move!"

Then a cry came from behind the door. "Hepzibah, Hepzibah, go down on the floor! Kiss his feet! I don't want to see him! Please!"

The Judge moved to the door. His face was angry. "Is he going to hit Hepzibah?" Phoebe thought.

Suddenly he stopped, and he smiled.

"Of course," Judge Pyncheon said, "Clifford isn't well. Maybe we can talk later. Goodbye!"

Hepzibah's face was white, and she took Phoebe's hand.

"Oh, Phoebe!" she said. "I can never love that man. When am I going to say it to his face?"

"Is he very bad?" Phoebe asked.

"Go now and talk to Clifford," Hepzibah said. "I'm going to work in the store."

Phoebe went to Clifford. "Is Judge Pyncheon bad?" she thought. "But he's an important man!"

Chapter 4   House and Garden

In the mornings, Clifford liked to sleep. Phoebe worked in the store and Hepzibah stayed with Clifford. In the afternoons, Hepzibah worked in the store and Phoebe stayed with Clifford. Phoebe often took Clifford into the garden. They talked about the flowers and she liked reading to him. He was happy there, with his young cousin.

The three cousins were usually in the garden on Sunday

"Of course," Judge Pyncheon said, "Clifford isn't well. Maybe we can talk later. Goodbye!"

afternoons. Holgrave and Mr. Venner often came, too.

One day Mr. Venner said, "Miss Hepzibah, I like meeting you here on Sundays. One day you can come and visit me in my house in the country."

"Mr. Venner is always talking about his 'house in the country,'" Clifford said, "but it's very, very small."

"We would all like a house in the country," Phoebe said.

And Phoebe was right. They loved the garden. It was their place in the sun.

But Phoebe and Clifford did not always go to the garden. Sometimes they went up to a room with a big window. It looked down on the street. They opened the window, and then Clifford watched the street. People came and went. Children played their games, and Clifford was happy. Or a train came, and he was afraid.

One day Clifford said, "I can hear music!" He moved near the window because he wanted to see. In the street, people walked to the music.

"I'm going to walk with them," Clifford thought. His foot was on the open window, and he started to go out. Hepzibah and Phoebe quickly stopped him.

"Clifford! What are you doing?" Hepzibah's face was white. Phoebe started to cry. "What's wrong with you?" Hepzibah asked.

"I don't know," Clifford said. "I wanted to be with people."

Phoebe was friendly with Holgrave. He was interesting, and she often talked with him about her family.

"How is Clifford?" Holgrave asked one day. He did not often see Clifford. "Is he happy?"

"Children are sometimes unhappy," Phoebe said. "Clifford is unhappy, too."

"Why?" Holgrave asked.

"I don't know," Phoebe answered. "I don't want to ask him about it. Why are you asking?"

"Because he's interesting," Holgrave answered. "I want to know about the Pyncheons. Do you know the story of the wizard Maule and Colonel Pyncheon?"

"Yes, I do," Phoebe answered. "Cousin Hepzibah talks about it. 'We're an unhappy family because the wizard cursed us,' Hepzibah says. What do you think?"

"Hepzibah is right!" Holgrave said. "And Colonel Pyncheon is with us again! Do you remember my picture? Was it a picture of Colonel Pyncheon or the Judge?"

"What are you saying?" Phoebe asked. "Are you sick?"

"I'm sorry," Holgrave said. His face was red, and he was quiet. Then he said, "I write stories. I have a story about the Pyncheons. Can I read it to you?"

Phoebe smiled at him. "Yes, I would like that."

Phoebe listened to his long story. It was about beautiful Alice Pyncheon, and Maule's curse. Phoebe's eyes were heavy, and they started to close.

Holgrave finished and looked at her. "Miss Phoebe," he said, "are you sleeping?"

"Me—sleeping?" Phoebe answered. "Of course not! I listened to your story. It was good."

"It's a beautiful evening," Holgrave said, "and now I'm happy. Tomorrow's a new day!"

"Yes, it is," Phoebe said. "But I'm not happy. Tomorrow I'm going to my mother's house. But only for a short time. My cousins need me, and this is my home now."

"You're right," Holgrave said. "They need you here."

"Are you afraid?" Phoebe asked. "What are you thinking?"

"I can't say," Holgrave answered. "But come back quickly. Goodbye, my friend!"

Phoebe went to her mother's house, and the House of the Seven Gables was dark again. Hepzibah had a lot of work in the store. But she was unhappy, and her customers started to stay away. Clifford was unhappy because Phoebe was not there. He only wanted to stay in bed. It was a difficult time for them.

One day, Judge Pyncheon came into the store. He smiled.

"How do you do, Cousin Hepzibah?" he said. "And how is Cousin Clifford? What do you need? Ask, and I can get it for you!"

"We don't need you," Hepzibah answered.

"But where is Clifford?" the Judge asked. "When is he going to meet his old friends?"

"You cannot see him," she answered. "He's in bed."

"Is he sick?" the Judge asked. "I'm going to see him. Maybe he's dead!"

"No, he isn't!" she said. "But you would like that!"

"Cousin Hepzibah," said the Judge. "You don't know me! I'm not a bad person. Clifford went to prison, but now he's home! Be happy!"

"Stop!" Hepzibah said. "You never loved my brother, and you don't love him now! Clifford went to prison because you wanted it!"

"Clifford is home again because I wanted it," the

Judge said quietly. "But I'm a judge, and I can put him back in prison! Now, take me to Clifford!"

"Never!" Hepzibah said. "Why are you doing this?"

"Cousin Hepzibah," the Judge said. "Do you remember the question about the Pyncheon land? Is it ours or not? Cousin Clifford has the answer! I want to ask him about it."

"You're wrong!" Hepzibah said.

"Take me to him, or I'm going to put him in prison again!" the Judge said.

Hepzibah looked at him. "The hair on your head is white, and you can only think about money! Maule's curse is working on you! I'm going to get Clifford. You're wrong, but you can hear it from him!"

They went from the store into the house. Hepzibah was afraid for Clifford. "But what can I do?" she thought. She opened the door to his bedroom.

"Clifford!" she called. But there was no answer. "Where is he? I'm going to the police," she thought. "No, first I'm going to find the Judge!" She went back.

Suddenly Clifford was there. His face was very white.

"Hepzibah," he said. "Now we can dance, now we can play! Look!"

Hepzibah went quickly into the room. There was Judge Pyncheon, dead in his chair!

"What are we going to do?" Hepzibah asked. She looked at her brother. He had his coat on.

"Come!" he said. "The Judge can have this old house!"

But Hepzibah was afraid, and did not move.

"Why are you waiting?" Clifford said. "Get your coat! Get your money! Come, Hepzibah!"

There was Judge Pyncheon, dead in his chair!

She started to move. "What am I doing?" she thought.

"Be quick!" Clifford said. "Or the dead can catch us!"

They went into the street. Clifford took his sister's hand, and they walked to the station.

"Get on the train," said Clifford.

"Which stop would you like?" the ticket man asked.

"It's not important," Clifford answered. "We like going on trains!"

The man took his money, and Clifford started to talk to people on the train.

"Clifford! Be quiet!" Hepzibah said.

"No!" Clifford answered. "For the first time in thirty years I can talk. I'm a new man!"

Chapter 5   Goodbye!

In the morning people came to the store, but it was closed. Where was Hepzibah? Then they started to ask about the Judge. Where was he? Phoebe arrived from the country. She tried the door to the store, but it did not open. She went to the front door. The schoolboy watched her from the street.

"Miss Phoebe!" he said. "Don't go in! It's bad!"

"Why is he running away?" Phoebe thought. The front door did not open. She went to the back door. She was afraid, but her hand was on the door. Suddenly it opened!

"It's Hepzibah!" thought Phoebe. She went in and the door closed behind her. It was dark. A hand took hers, and they walked into a big room. "But this isn't Hepzibah's hand!" Phoebe thought.

"Holgrave!" she said. He smiled at her, but his face was white. "Where are Hepzibah and Clifford? Why is the house quiet?" Phoebe asked.

"They aren't here," he answered.

"Where are they?" Phoebe said. "I'm going to find them."

"Wait!" Holgrave said. "Judge Pyncheon is dead. And he's sitting in Colonel Pyncheon's chair! I wanted to find Hepzibah, and there was the Judge, dead in his chair!"

Phoebe was afraid. "Did you call the police?" she asked.

"No," Holgrave said. "Clifford and Hepzibah went away. The police are going to want Clifford."

"Clifford!" Phoebe said.

"You don't know his story!" Holgrave said. "He went to prison for thirty years because Judge Pyncheon wanted him there. Clifford went to prison for the murder of his father's brother. But it wasn't murder! His father's brother had a bad heart, and Judge Pyncheon had a bad heart, too. *That's* the curse of the Pyncheon family!"

"Open the doors!" she said. "Then the town can hear."

"You're right," Holgrave said, but he did not move. He talked slowly. "Phoebe, I was here with the Judge. I looked into the dead man's eyes, and I thought about Clifford and his thirty years in prison. Thirty years! Phoebe, I'm not thirty years old! But then you came back. I took your hand, remember? Phoebe, I love you."

"How can you love me?" Phoebe asked. "We're not the same. How can we be happy?"

"I can only be happy with you!" Holgrave said.

"And I'm afraid," Phoebe said. She moved near to him.

"Phoebe, do you love me?" Holgrave asked.

Phoebe looked down. "Yes, I do," she said.

They were quiet, and happy. Then Phoebe asked, "What's that noise?"

"Maybe it's the police," Holgrave said.

"Brother, we're home!" It was Hepzibah. "And here is our little Phoebe—and Holgrave, too!"

They went to the police, and doctors came to the house.

"Yes, the Judge had a bad heart," they said.

One day, Hepzibah, Clifford, and Phoebe were in the room with Colonel Pyncheon's picture. Holgrave and Mr. Venner were there, too.

"Clifford," Hepzibah said, "now the Judge's money and his big country house are ours. But is *this* house and the Pyncheon land ours, too? Do you know the answer?"

Clifford smiled. "Ah, the Pyncheon land. Don't think about it, Hepzibah. We don't need it."

"You're right," Holgrave said. "And it isn't your land."

"But how do you know?" Phoebe asked.

Holgrave looked at her. "My family knows," he said. "I'm a Maule—but I'm not a wizard!"

"We're going to move to the Judge's country house," Phoebe said. "Mr. Venner, please come and live with us. We have a big garden there. Would you like that?"

"Yes!" he said.

They closed the House of the Seven Gables and moved to the country. Phoebe took some flowers with her. They were Alice's Flowers.

ACTIVITIES

Chapter 1

Before you read

1 Read the Introduction to this book. What do you know about Hepzibah and her brother?

2 Look at the Word List at the back of the book. Answer the questions.

   a What are you *afraid* of?

   b What do you do with a *biscuit*?

   c How many *cousins* do you have?

   d Where can you see a *wizard*?

While you read

3 What do you know? What do you think? Write Yes in the right places.

	good	bad	old	young
a Hepzibah Pyncheon	✓		✓	
b Mr. Holgrave	✓			✓
c Judge Pyncheon		✓	✓	
d Colonel Pyncheon				
e Mr. Venner	✓			
f Phoebe Pyncheon	✓			✓

After you read

4 Are these sentences about the Pyncheons right or wrong?

   a Miss Hepzibah Pyncheon has a lot of money. ✗

   b Judge Pyncheon is Hepzibah's father.

   c Colonel Pyncheon is dead.

   d Matthew Maule is a good friend of the Pyncheon family. ✗

   e Clifford is one of Phoebe's cousins. ✓

25

Chapter 2

Before you read

5 What do you think? Talk to a friend.

    a Who is going to help Hepzibah in the store?

    b Is Hepzibah going to make money from the store?

    c Who is going to come home to the House of the Seven Gables?

While you read

6 Find the right answer.

    a Phoebe likes the *white/black* flowers in the garden.

    b Hepzibah's small picture is of *an old/a young* man.

    c People in the Pyncheon family *usually have/do not have* jobs.

    d Phoebe *likes/does not like* Colonel Pyncheon's face.

    e Hepzibah is *sometimes/always* afraid of Mr. Holgrave.

    f Mr. Holgrave *writes books/takes pictures*.

    g The man in Mr. Holgrave's picture has a *friendly/cold* face.

After you read

7 Talk to a friend. What makes these people happy or unhappy?

Hepzibah Phoebe Mr. Holgrave

Chapter 3

Before you read

8 What do you think? Talk to a friend.

    a Which man is going to love Phoebe one day?

    b Who are the men in Hepzibah's and Mr. Holgrave's pictures?

While you read

9 Who is it? Write Clifford, Phoebe, or the Judge.

    a She is Arthur's daughter. ....

    b He is Hepzibah's brother. ....

c He is an important, fat man. ....

d He is the man in Holgrave's picture. ....

e He is afraid of Judge Pyncheon. ....

After you read

10 Talk about Clifford Pyncheon and Judge Pyncheon.

　　a When and why is Judge Pyncheon friendly or angry?

　　b When and why is Clifford happy, quiet, or afraid?

Chapter 4

Before you read

11 Which people in the story do you like? Why?

While you read

12 What comes first? Write 1–7.

　　a Judge Pyncheon is dead in his chair. .....

　　b Holgrave reads his story to Phoebe. .....

　　c Phoebe goes to her mother's house for a visit. .....

　　d Hepzibah and Clifford get on a train. .....

　　e Judge Pyncheon comes into Hepzibah's store. .....

　　f Mr. Holgrave and Phoebe talk about the curse. .....

After you read

13 Why . . . ?

　　a would the Pyncheons like a house in the country?

　　b do Phoebe and Hepzibah watch Clifford all the time?

　　c did Clifford go to prison?

　　d does Judge Pyncheon want to talk to Clifford?

　　e do Clifford and Hepzibah get on a train?

Chapter 5

Before you read

14 Tell a story about a family with problems. Are the problems about money, houses, land, or a curse?

15 Is the Judge dead at this time or not? Write Before or After.

    a Hepzibah's store is open. ....

    b Holgrave takes Phoebe's hand. ....

    c The House of the Seven Gables is quiet. ....

    d Clifford is in prison. ....

    e The doctors look at the Judge in his chair. ....

After you read

16 Talk about these questions.

    a Was there a curse on the Pyncheon family? Why (not)?

    b Are the Pyncheons going to be happy now? Why (not)?

Writing

17 You are Phoebe before this story. You want to visit the House of the Seven Gables. Write a letter to your cousin Hepzibah about your visit.

18 You are Clifford Pyncheon. Write a story for the newspaper: "My Thirty Years in Prison".

19 You are Phoebe Pyncheon, and you love Mr. Holgrave. Write a letter to your mother about him.

20 Judge Pyncheon is dead. You are a policeman, and you went to the House of the Seven Gables. Write about the dead man for the police.

21 Write a story about the Pyncheon family in their big house in the country.

22 Holgrave is talking to his children. His daughter asks, "How did you meet Mother?" Write Holgrave's answer.